Copyright © Daniel Jones 2025

www.anchor-lines.com

First published 2025 by Malcolm Down Publishing Ltd.

www.malcolmdown.co.uk

The right of Daniel Jones to be identified as the author of this work has been asserted by him in accordance with the Copyright, Designs and Patents Act 1988.

All rights reserved. No part of this publication may be reproduced, stored in a retrieval system, or transmitted in any other form or by any means, electronic, mechanical, photocopying, recording or otherwise, without the prior permission of the publisher.

British Library Cataloguing in Publication Data

A catalogue record for this book is available from the British Library.

ISBN 978-1-917455-47-3

Cover design by Daniel Jones

Printed in the UK

This poem is based on 'The Celestial Country' – written in Latin by a monk named Bernard de Cluny in the French Abbey of Cluny around 1145 AD, and translated into English by Dr. John Mason Neale in 1851 AD.

I first read this poem shortly after the death of my first wife, Ali, who went to be with the Lord at 37 years old following a sudden and unexpected cancer diagnosis. It is a profound and deeply moving call to hope, and over the last two years I have updated and illustrated it to share it with others.

The central theme of the poem is the great promise we have of eternal life with God, beginning now and growing brighter and more beautiful when our time here ends or when Jesus returns. Jesus speaks to us of reward, of paradise, of wedding feasts and of joy. If you struggle to imagine or think much about the life to come, this illustrated poem is intended to help you grow in excitement and anticipation of what God has promised us in heaven.

If following Jesus is at times hard – if our pilgrimage in this world is at times challenging – the encouragement we need is to know that not only are we serving the Lord, and not only is Christ with us now, but that whatever trials we face for his sake are storing up for us something greater by far.

May God help you to know better the extraordinary hope to which he has called you.

At the end of the book, I have included a full copy of the original poem along with some questions that could be used for a personal or group study.

THE WORLD IS FULL OF EVIL

THE HOUR IS GROWING LATE

STAY SOBER AND BE WATCHFUL:

THE JUDGE IS AT THE GATE

THE JUDGE WHO COMES WITH MERCY

THE JUDGE WHO COMES WITH MIGHT

TO MAKE AN END OF EVIL

TO SET THE WORLD TO RIGHT

THE JUST AND GENTLE MONARCH SHALL CALL OUR BONES TO STAND

LET GUILTY MORTALS TREMBLE LEST THEY FALL INTO HIS HAND

AND THOSE WHO WAIT IN PARADISE
WILL NO MORE SLEEP IN DEATH

HE SPEAKS, EACH SOUL WILL RISE TO LIFE
AND DRAW THEIR FIRST NEW BREATH

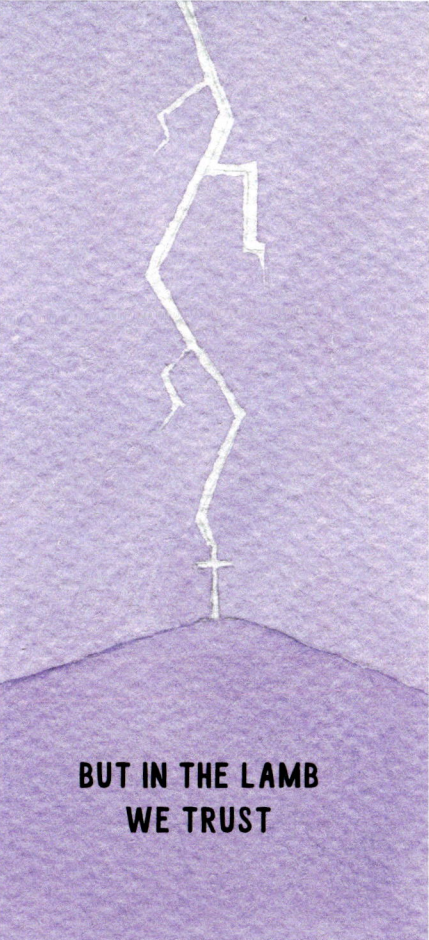

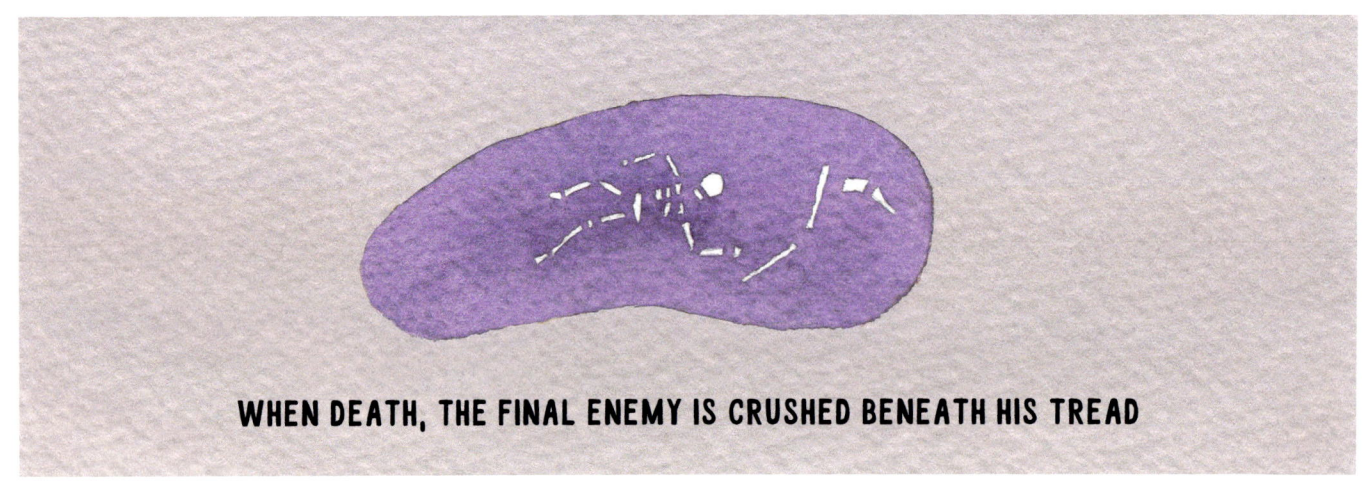

WHEN CHRIST RETURNS THE KINGDOM
TO HIS FATHER AS HE SAID

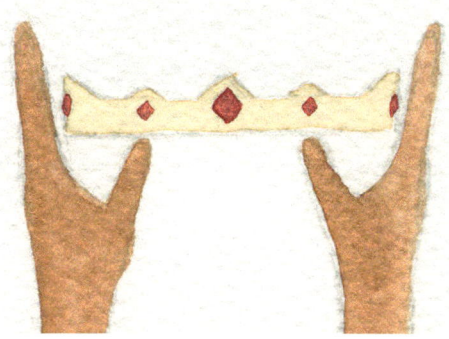

THEN GLORIES YET UNHEARD OF
SHALL BLAZE FROM EAST TO WEST

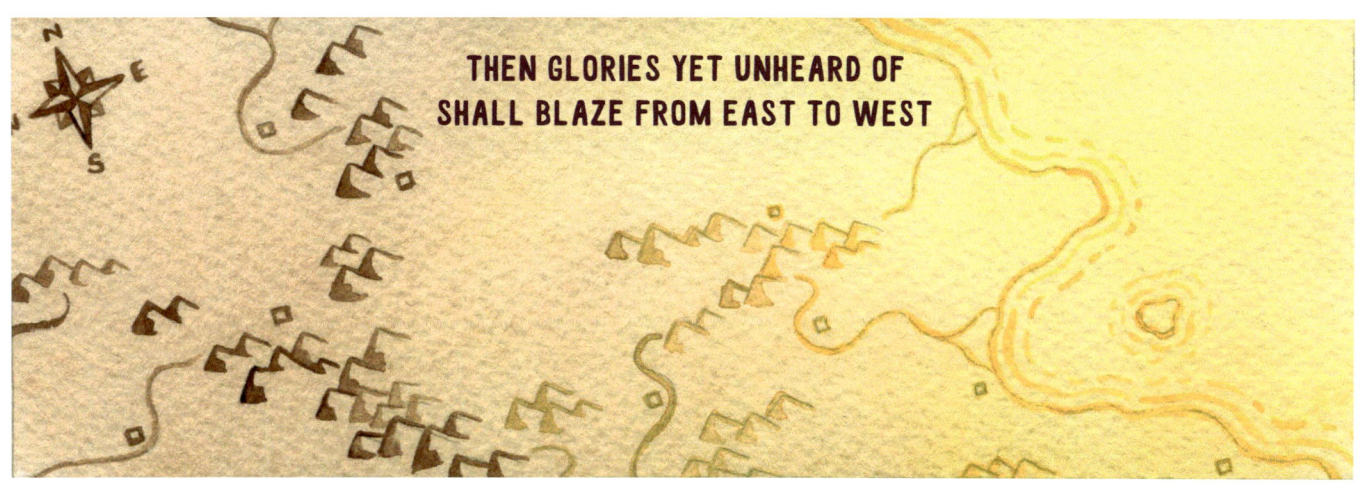

ALL QUESTIONS FIND THEIR ANSWERS
IN THAT ENDLESS DAY OF REST

THE FALLEN AND THE FAITHFUL

THE LOST - AND THOSE WHO STAND

THE GOAT HERD AND THE SHEEP FLOCK
WILL PART WAYS ON EITHER HAND

WHERE WE WILL BE HIS PEOPLE

AND HE WILL GLADLY DWELL

AND EVER HAVE THE PRESENCE
OF OUR LORD EMMANUEL

WHERE GRIEF IS TURNED TO PLEASURE, SUCH PLEASURE AS BELOW

NO HUMAN VOICE CAN UTTER

NO HUMAN HEART CAN KNOW

HIS PEACE THAT FILLS THE FAITHFUL

HIS CALM THAT FILLS THE BLESSED

THERE, NOTHING CAN BE FEEBLE 	**THERE, NOTHING CAN BE TORN** 
THERE, NOTHING IS DIVIDED  	**THERE, NONE CAN EVER MOURN** 

YES, PEACE! FOR WAR IS OVER

YES, CALM! THE STORM IS PAST

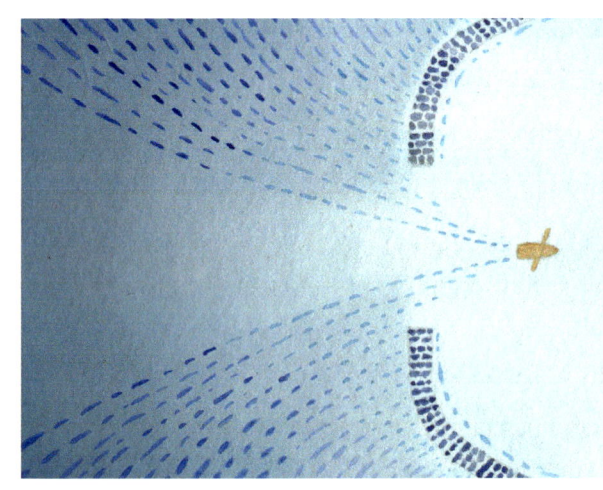

AND REST FROM FINISHED LABOUR AND SAFE ANCHORAGE AT LAST

AND AFTER SIN & SCANDAL!

AND AFTER THIS WORLD'S NIGHT

AFTER STORM AND WHIRLWIND
IS CALM, AND JOY, AND LIGHT

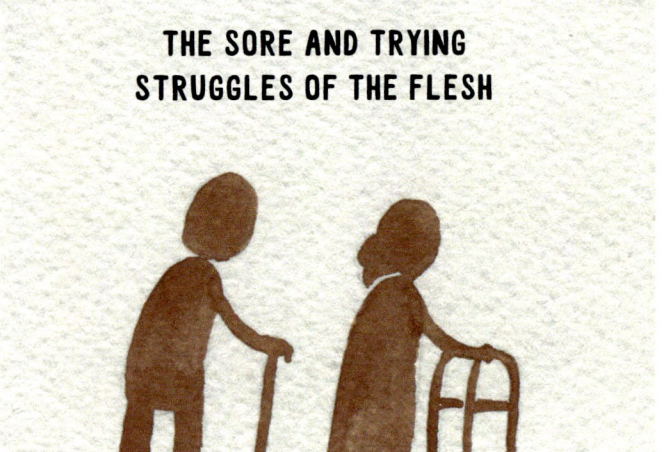 

TILL WE SHOULD REACH THAT MOUNTAINTOP
WHERE JESUS' FEAST IS SET

WHERE ALL DESIRES ARE GOOD DESIRES
AND EACH OF THEM IS MET!

FOR ALL SHALL
BE RECOVERED
AND ALL SHALL
BE COMPLETE

AND IN THE
LAND OF BEAUTY,
ALL THINGS OF
BEAUTY MEET

BY FAITH WE JOURNEY ONWARD
TO THE LAND FOR WHICH WE LONG

NOW LEANING IN OUR WEAKNESS ON HIM WHO'S EVER

STRONG

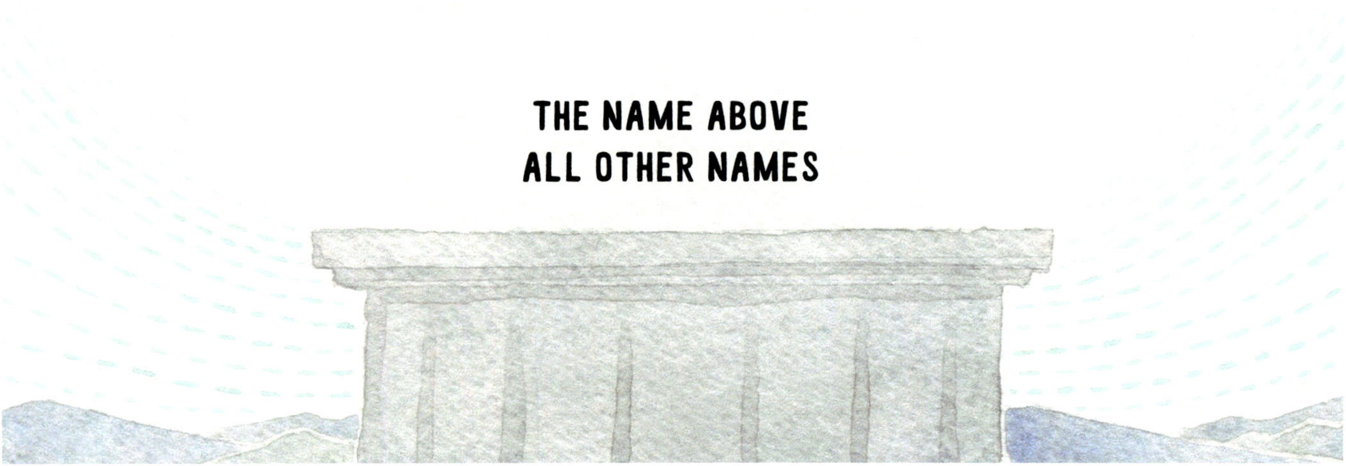

AND THOUGH THE NIGHT IS DARK,
AND THOUGH ITS TERRORS LEAVE YOU WORN

KNOW THIS, HE WILL RETURN
TO BRING US TRIUMPH WITH THE DAWN

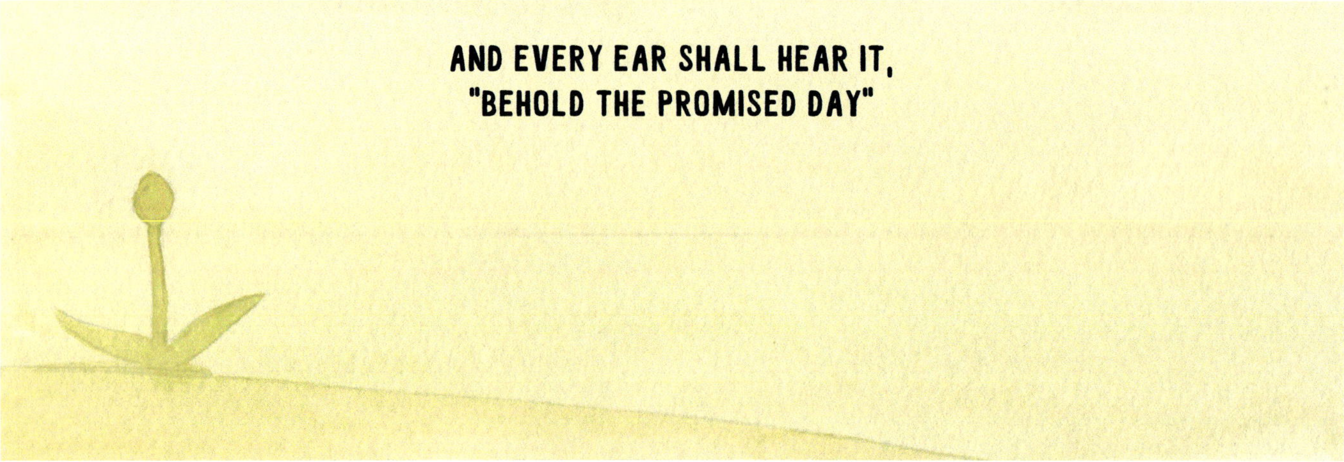

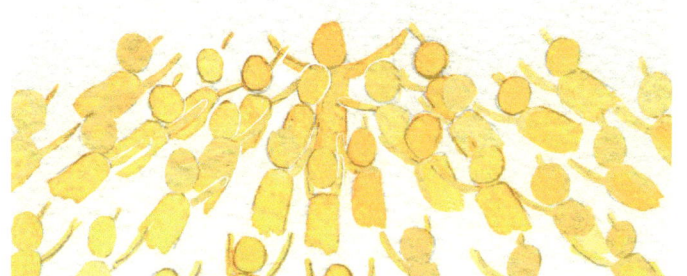

THE CEDAR OF THE FOREST

THE HYSSOP OF THE WALL

THE TREES OF LIFE RISE GOLDEN FROM THEIR EVER-LIVING ROOTS

WITH HEALING FOR THE NATIONS IN THEIR BOUGHS AND LEAVES AND SHOOTS

OH CITADEL
OF FLOWERS,
OH CITY
RICH WITH GREEN,

ABLAZE WITH BRILLIANT COLOUR
LIKE NO GARDEN EVER SEEN

THE LAND WHERE HOME AND NATURE
BOTH CAN JOYFULLY EXIST

NO JUNGLE ON THE EARTH
COULD BURST WITH SO MUCH LIFE AS THIS

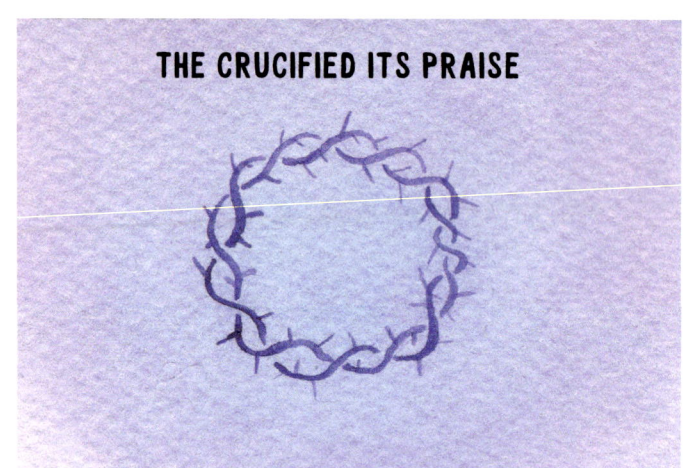

THE NEVER FAILING GARDEN

THE EVER GOLDEN RING

THE BREAD THAT COMES FROM HEAVEN

THE BRIDEGROOM TO HIS WIFE

THE DOOR

THE RESURRECTION

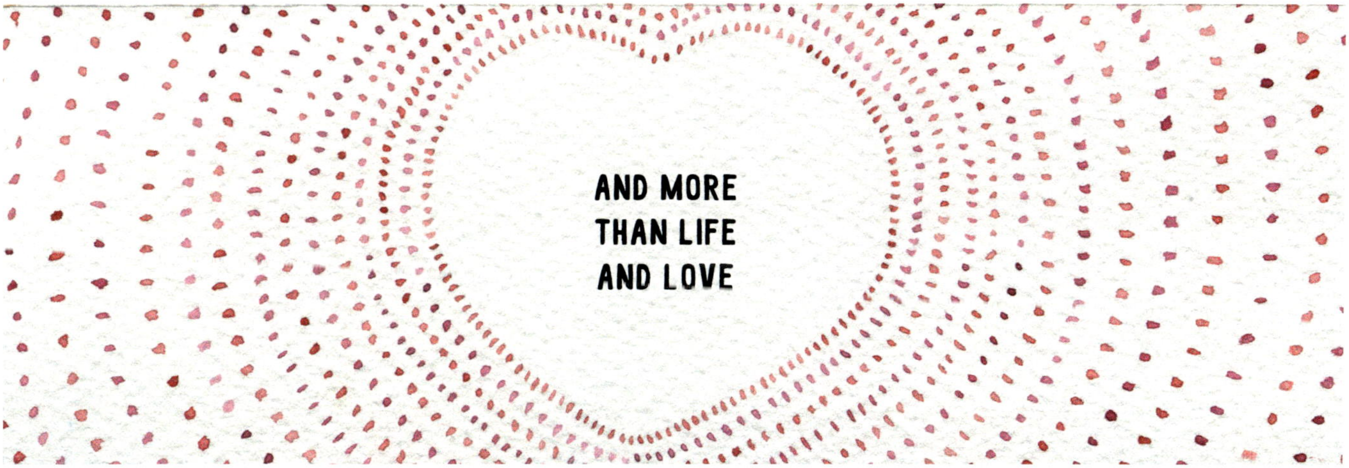

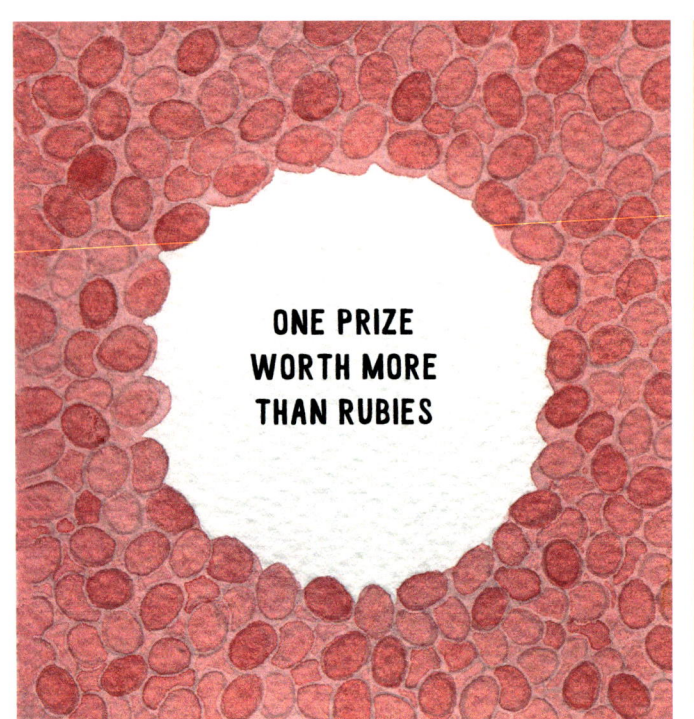

GOD'S PRESENCE IS THE VERY

AND NOW OUR HEARTS
HAVE HEARD OF IT
NO OTHER HOME WILL DO

WE ASK NO
OTHER PARADISE
EXCEPT IT BE
WITH YOU

I ASK NOT FOR MY MERIT

I SEEK NOT TO DENY

THE BATTLE HAS BEEN WON

THE SPIRIT LIVING IN US AND THE WAITING BRIDE SAY, "COME!"

The Celestial Country

Dr. John Mason Neale's 1851 translation of Bernard de Cluny's original

The world is very evil,
The times are waxing late;
Be sober and keep vigil,
The Judge is at the gate.
The Judge that comes in mercy,
The Judge that comes with might,
To terminate the evil,
To diadem the right.
When the just and gentle Monarch
Shall summon from the tomb,
Let man, the guilty, tremble,
For Man, the God, shall doom

Arise, arise, good Christian,
Let right to wrong succeed;
Let penitential sorrow
To heavenly gladness lead;
To the light that hath no evening,
That knows nor moon nor sun,
The light so new and golden,
The light that is but one.

And when the Sole-Begotten
Shall render up once more
The Kingdom to the Father,
Whose own it was before,
Then glory yet unheard of
Shall shed abroad its ray,
Resolving all enigmas,
An endless Sabbath-day.

Then, then from his oppressors
The Hebrew shall go free,
And celebrate in triumph
The year of Jubilee;
And the sunlit Land that recks not
Of tempest nor of fight,
Shall fold within its bosom
Each happy Israelite:
The Home of fadeless splendor,
Of flowers that fear no thorn,
Where they shall dwell as children,
Who here as exiles mourn.

Midst power that knows no limit,
And wisdom free from bound,
The Beatific Vision
Shall glad the saints around:
The peace of all the faithful,
The calm of all the blest,
Inviolate, unvaried,
Divinest, sweetest, best.
Yes, peace! for war is needless,
Yes, calm! for storm is past,
And goal from finished labor
And anchorage at last.

That peace—but who may claim it?
The guileless in their way,
Who keep the ranks of battle,
Who mean the thing they say:

The peace that is for heaven,
And shall be too, for earth:
The palace that re-echoes
With festal song and mirth;
The garden, breathing spices,
The paradise on high;
Grace beautified to glory,
Unceasing minstrelsy.

There nothing can be feeble,
There none can ever mourn,
There nothing is divided,
There nothing can be torn.
'Tis fury, ill, and scandal,
'Tis peaceless peace below;
Peace, endless, strifeless, ageless,
The halls of Syon* know.

O happy, holy portion,
Refection for the blest;
True vision of true beauty,
Sweet cure of all distrest!
Strive, man, to win that glory,
Toil, man, to gain that light;
Send hope before to grasp it,
Till hope be lost in sight:
Till Jesus gives the portion
Those blessed souls to fill,
The insatiate, yet satisfied,
The full, yet craving still.

That fulness and that craving
Alike are free from pain,
Where thou, 'midst heavenly citizens,
A home like theirs shall gain.

Here is the warlike trumpet;
There, life set free from sin;
When to the last Great Supper
The faithful shall come in:
When the heavenly net is laden
With fishes many and great;
So glorious in its fullness,
Yet so inviolate:
And the perfect from the shattered,
And the fall'n from them that stand,
And the sheep-flock from the goat-herd
Shall part on either hand:
And these shall pass to torment,
And those shall triumph then,
The new peculiar nation,
Blest number of blest men.

Jerusalem demands them:
They paid the price on earth,
And now shall reap the harvest
In blissfulness and mirth:
The glorious holy people,
Who evermore relied
Upon their Chief and Father,
The King, the Crucified:
The sacred ransomed number
Now bright with endless sheen,
Who made the Cross their watchword
Of Jesus Nazarene:
Who, fed with heavenly nectar,
Where soul-like odors play,
Draw out the endless leisure
Of that long vernal day.

*Syon - an alternative spelling of Zion

While through the sacred lilies,
And flowers on every side,
The happy dear-bought people
Go wandering far and wide.
Their breasts are filled with gladness,
Their mouths are tuned to praise,
What time, now safe forever,
On former sins they gaze:
The fouler was the error,
The sadder was the fall,
The ampler are the praises
Of Him who pardoned all.

Their one and only anthem,
The fulness of His love,
Who gives instead of torment,
Eternal joys above:
Instead of torment, glory;
Instead of death, that life
Wherewith your happy Country,
True Isarelites! is rife.

Brief life is here our portion;
Brief sorrow, short-lived care:
The life that knows no ending,
The tearless life, is There.

O happy retribution!
Short toil, eternal rest;
For mortals and for sinner
A mansion with the blest!
That we should look, poor wand'rers,
To have our home on high!
That worms should seek for dwellings
Beyond the starry sky!

To all one happy guerdon*
Of one celestial grace;
For all, for all, who mourn their fall,
Is one eternal place.

And martyrdom hath roses
Upon that heavenly ground:
And white and virgin lilies
For virgin-souls abound.
There grief is tamed to pleasure;
Such pleasure, as below
No human voice can utter,
No human heart can know.
And after fleshly scandal,
And after this world's night,
And after storm and whirlwind
Is calm, and joy, and light.

And now we fight the battle,
But then shall wear the crown
Of full and everlasting
And passionless renown:
And now we watch and struggle
And now we live in hope,
And Syon, in her anguish,
With Babylon must cope:
But He Whom now we trust in
Shall then be seen and known,
And they that know and see Him
Shall have Him for their own.

The miserable pleasures
Of the body shall decay:
The bland and flattering struggles
Of the flesh shall pass away:

* Guerdon – a reward

And none shall there be jealous;
And none shall there contend:
Fraud, clamor, guile—what say I?—
All ill, all ill shall end!

And there is David's Fountain,
And life in fullest glow,
And there the light is golden,
And milk and honey flow:
The light that hath no evening,
The health that hath no sore,
The life that hath no ending,
But lasteth evermore.

There Jesus shall embrace us,
There Jesus be embraced,—
That spirit's food and sunshine
Whence meaner love is chased.
Amidst the happy chorus,
A place, however low,
Shall show Him us; and showing,
Shall satiate evermo.

By hope we straggle onward,
While here we most be fed
With milk, as tender infants,
But there with Living Bread.

The night was full of terror,
The morn is bright with gladness,
The Cross becomes our harbor,
And we triumph after sadness;

And Jesus to His true ones
Brings trophies fair to see:

And Jesus shall be loved, and
Beheld in Galilee.
Beheld, when morn shall waken,
And shadows shall decay,
And each true-hearted servant
Shall shine as doth the day:
And every ear shall hear it;—
Behold thy King's array;
Behold thy God in beauty;
The Law hath passed away!
Yes! God, my King and Portion,
In fulness of His grace,
We then shall see forever,
And worship face to face.

Then Jacob into Israel,
From earthlier self estranged,
And Leah into Rachel
Forever shall be changed:
Then all the halls of Syon
For aye shall be complete;
And, in the Land of Beauty,
All things of beauty meet.

For thee, O dear, dear Country!
Mine eyes their vigils keep;
For very love, beholding
Thy happy name, they weep;
The mention of thy glory
Is unction to the breast,
And medicine in sickness,
And love, and life, and rest.

O one, O only Mansion!
O Paradise of Joy!

Where tears are ever banished,
And smiles have no alloy;
Beside thy living waters
All plants are, great and small,
The cedar of the forest,
The hyssop of the wall.
With jaspers glow thy bulwarks;
Thy streets with emeralds blaze;
The sardius and the topaz
Unite in thee their rays:
Thine ageless walls are bounded
With amethyst unpriced;
Thy saints build up its fabric,
And the corner-stone is Christ.

The Cross is all thy splendor,
The Crucified thy praise;
His laud and benediction
Thy ransomed people raise;
Jesus, the Gem of Beauty,
True God and Man, they sing;
The never-failing Garden,
The ever-golden Ring:
The Door, the Pledge, the Husband,
The Guardian of His Court;
The Day-star of Salvation,
The Porter and the Port!

Thou hast no shore, fair ocean!
Thou has no time, bright day!
Dear fountain of refreshment
To pilgrims far away!
Upon the Rock of Ages
They raise thy holy tower:
Thine is the victor's laurel,
And thine the golden dower.

Thou feel'st in mystic rapture,
O Bride, that knowest no guile,
The Prince's sweetest kisses,
The Prince's loveliest smile:
Unfading lilies, bracelets
Of living pearl, thine own;
The Lamb is ever near thee,
The Bridegroom thine alone;
The Crown is He to guerdon,
The Buckler to protect,
And He Himself the Mansion,
And He the Architect.

The only art thou needest,
Thanksgiving for thy lot:
The only joy thou seekest,
The Life where Death is not.
And all thine endless leisure
In sweetest accents sings,
The ill that was thy merit,
The wealth that is thy King's!

Jerusalem the Golden,
With milk and honey blest,
Beneath thy contemplation
Sink heart and voice oppressed:
I know not, O, I know not,
What social joys are there;
What radiancy of glory,
What light beyond compare!

And when I fain would sing them,
My spirit falls and faints,

And vainly would it image
The assembly of the Saints.

They stand, those halls of Syon,
Conjubilant with song,
And bright with many an angel,
And all the martyr throng;
The Prince is ever in them,
The daylight is serene;
The pastures of the blessed
Are decked in glorious sheen.

There is the throne of David,
And there, from care released,
The song of them that triumph,
The shouts of them that feast;
And they who, with their Leader,
Have conquered in the fight,
Forever and forever
Are clad in robes of white.

O holy, placid harp-notes
Of that eternal hymn!
O sacred sweet reflection,
And peace of Seraphim!
O thirst, forever ardent,
Yet evermore content!
O true, peculiar vision
Of God cunctipotent!*

Ye know the many mansions
For many a glorious name,
And diverse retributions
That diverse merits claim:
For 'midst the constellations

That deck our earthly sky,
This star than that is brighter
And so it is on high.

Jerusalem the glorious
The glory of the Elect!
O dear and future vision
That eager hearts expect:
Even now by faith I see thee:
Even here thy walls discern:
To thee my thoughts are kindled,
And strive and pant and yearn!

Jerusalem the only,
That look'st from heaven below
In thee is all my glory;
In me is all my woe;
And though my body may not,
My spirit seeks thee fain,
Till flesh and earth return me
To earth and flesh again.

Oh, none can tell thy bulwarks
How gloriously they rise;
Oh, none can tell thy capitals
Of beautiful device;
Thy loveliness oppresses
All human thought and heart:
And none, O peace, O Syon,
Can sing thee as thou art.

New mansion of new people,
Whom God's own love and light
Promote, increase, make holy,
Identify, unite.

* Another word for omnipotent; all-powerful

Thou City of the Angels!
Thou City of the Lord!
Whose everlasting music
Is the glorious decachord!

And there the band of Prophets
United praise ascribes,
And there the twelvefold chorus
Of Israel's ransomed tribes:
The lily-beds of virgins,
The roses' martyr-glow,
The cohort of the Fathers
Who kept the faith below.

And there the Sole-Begotten
Is Lord in regal state;
He, Judah's mystic Lion,
He, Lamb Immaculate.
O fields that know no sorrow!
O state that fears no strife!
O princely bow'rs! O land of flow'rs!
O Realm and Home of Life!

Jerusalem, exulting
On that securest shore,
I hope thee, wish thee, sing thee,
And love thee evermore!
I ask not for my merit:
I seek not to deny
My merit is destruction,
A child of wrath am I:
But yet with Faith I venture
And Hope upon my way;
For those perennial guerdons
I labor night and day.

The Best and Dearest Father
Who made me and Who saved.
Bore with me in defilement,
And from defilement laved*,
When in His strength I struggle,
For very joy I leap;
When in my sin I totter,
I weep, or try to weep:
And grace, sweet grace celestial
Shall all its love display,
And David's Royal Fountain
Purge every sin away.

O mine, my golden Syon!
O lovelier far than gold!
With laurel-girt battalions,
And safe victorious fold:
O sweet and blessed Country,
Shall I ever see thy face?
O sweet and blessed Country,
Shall I ever will thy grace?
I have the hope within me
To comfort and to bless!
Shall I ever win the prize itself?
O tell me, tell me, yes!

Exult, O dust and ashes!
The Lord shall be thy part;
His only, His forever,
Thou shalt be, and thou art!
Exult, O dust and ashes!
The Lord shall be thy part:
His only, His forever,
Thou shalt be, and thou art!

* Laved - washed

For reflection:

How often do you think about the life to come? Is it something that gives you hope and that you look forward to, or something you rarely think about?

Many people find it hard to look forward to heaven with hope. For some it's really hard to imagine anything of what it might be like. For some it seems too far off to be relevant to the real demands of everyday life. For some it can be worrying, thinking of a life that's different to what we now know. What about you?

Here are some passages that speak about eternal life and the promise of the new heavens and earth. Pick one to read through and discuss, or write down some things that stand out to you:

- John 17:3
- 1 Corinthians 15
- Revelation 21:1-22:5
- 2 Corinthians 4
- Philippians 1:19-24
- Luke 23:39-43

Paradise with God – whether now when we die, or when Jesus returns to make all things new – is meant to be a joy and comfort to us. What helps you to take hold of that hope? Are there particular bible verses? Songs? Pictures or poems?

What parts of the poem (whether the original or the illustrated one) stood out to you? How did they make you feel?

What is it about life after death that you most look forward to? There doesn't have to be just one answer, you can give several!

WOLF to WHOODLE